AWAKE YOUR WEALT

Workbook

JULIE MARIE MURPHY, CFP®

Using a workbook is a great way to track your day-to-day experiences and record your progress through a course. I've designed this workbook to accompany my online course, giving you a space to write down your thoughts and reflections as you go through the Awaken Your Wealth lessons. Please be sure to carry the workbook with you and write what comes to mind, even if that means simply jotting down some ideas or notes to yourself.

I hope that you find this experience as enjoyable and rewarding as I have, as you work through the PACT process!

Julie✤

Table of Contents

1 Lesson One Activities

After completing Lesson One, take a few minutes to reflect on what each step in the PACT process means to you, and write down some of your thoughts.

P *Picturing Yourself*

_____

_____

_____

A *Accepting Reality and Awakening*

_____

_____

_____

C *Choosing to Change*

_____

_____

_____

T *Taking Action*

_____

_____

_____

Ideas and Strategies: *Please work through these exercises before you start Lesson 2. Remember, it's all about having financial fun!*

Permission to Spend: What have you wanted to buy, or a place you wanted to travel to? Use these items to reward yourself along the way for good behavior. You've stuck to your plan, so give yourself a reward.

_____

_____

_____

_____

_____

_____

_____

_____

Attitude Towards Money: Where do you fall on the spectrum from financial scarcity to financial abundance? What changes can you make to create a different, more desired, financial future?

Scarcity	Hybrid	Abundance

_____

_____

_____

_____

_____

_____

_____

_____

Emotions: Write down some of the emotions you may have around your money.

_____

_____

_____

_____

_____

_____

_____

_____

_____

Meditation: Use this section to write down intentional times that you will meditate, and for how many minutes. Then, keep track of your progress!

Sunday _____

Monday _____

Tuesday _____

Wednesday _____

Thursday _____

Friday _____

Saturday _____

_____

_____

_____

Innate Body Intelligence/ Core Beliefs:

Pay attention to your emotional reactions around money, career, earnings, and savings.

Whenever you feel anxious about money, make notes to help identify your own personal patterns.

Positive Thinking: Write down words that you feel best describe each of these four core beliefs — what they are and where they come from:

Love _____
_____
_____
_____
_____

Self-Worth _____
_____
_____
_____

Wholeness _____
_____
_____
_____

Safety _____
_____
_____
_____

Remember—An important first step is to begin turning any negative thinking into the positive. When you catch yourself using vocabulary that seems to be more reactive and alarming than productive, re-frame it. The goal is to internalize a positive approach to your thinking and speaking.

Feminine and Masculine Energies:

We strategize our inner world with our feminine side and decipher the outer world with our masculine side. Are both sides working in concert with each other for you? Think about when you last experienced each of these energies.

Write down your thoughts.

2 Lesson Two Activities
Picturing Yourself

Become a dream maker! *Write your answers to the following questions as you work through Lesson Two:*

♥ *Where would you like to see yourself in three to five years? Include any elements that come to mind about your life, including work, family, financial, or personal.*

_____

_____

_____

_____

♥ *What are your coworkers like? What is your boss like? If you are self-employed, what is your workday like?*

_____

_____

_____

_____

♥ *At your job, what would you love to do daily? Is that what you did today at work?*

_____

_____

_____

♥ *Why did you choose your current career path? Does it excite you today?*

_____

_____

_____

♥ *When you were a child, what were your dreams?*
  What creates happiness for you today?

_____

_____

_____

♥ *What have you always wanted to do? Do you have any regrets?*

_____

_____

_____

♥ *What desires have you been negotiating away due to "life circumstances?"*

_____

_____

_____

♥ *From a family life perspective, what have you always been drawn to?*

_____

_____

_____

♥ *What is on your back-burner? What keeps you from doing it?*

_____

_____

_____

♥ *Do people tell you that you are crazy for thinking the way you do?*
  Excellent! Then you're being authentic!

_____

_____

_____

♥ *What physical ailments or mental blocks are concerning you?*

_____

_____

_____

_____

♥ *Why do you want these things or experiences?*

_____

_____

_____

♥ *What motivates you — your personal, compelling reason?*

_____

_____

_____

♥ *What do you love?*

_____

_____

_____

♥ *What would actually make you happier?*

_____

_____

_____

_____

♥ *What makes you giggle, or smile?*

_____

_____

_____

♥ *What feels life-supporting and expansive?*

♥ *What makes you feel alive and energized?*

Notes

Work Life

♥ How does your work life feel?

_____

_____

♥ Do certain responsibilities make you uncomfortable?

_____

_____

♥ Do you get excited or energized by where you are now?

_____

_____

♥ Is there something missing in your work?

_____

_____

♥ Do you long for or seek something else?

_____

_____

♥ Can you describe what you are looking for?

_____

_____

♥ What would you most love to change about your job that's affecting your personal, financial, or family life?

_____

_____

♥ What else?

_____

_____

Family Life

♥ *How does your family life feel?*

♥ *Do certain family members or responsibilities make you uncomfortable?*

♥ *Do you get excited or energized by this facet of your life?*

♥ *Is there something missing in your family life?*

♥ *Do you long for or seek a new family dynamic?*

♥ *Can you describe what that new family dynamic would look like?*

♥ *What would you most love to change about family life, if anything?*

♥ *What else?*

Personal Life

♥ How does your personal life feel?

_____

_____

♥ Do certain aspects of your family life make you feel uncomfortable?

_____

_____

♥ Do you get excited or energized by where you are now personally?

_____

_____

♥ Is there something missing in your personal life?

_____

_____

♥ Do you long for or seek something else in your personal life to feed your soul?

_____

_____

♥ Can you describe what you are looking for? What would make you giggle?

_____

_____

♥ What would you most love to change about personal life?

_____

_____

_____

♥ What else?

_____

_____

_____

Financial Life

♥ *How do you feel about your money situation?*

♥ *Do certain aspects or responsibilities make you uncomfortable financially?*

♥ *Do you get excited or energized by where you are now with your money?*

♥ *Is there something missing in your financial life?*

♥ *Do you long for or seek a new financial reality?*

♥ *Can you describe what you are looking for?*

♥ *What would you most love to change about your financial life?*

♥ *What else?*

Lesson Three Activities
Accepting Reality and Awakening

The Economic Choice Points: *After exploring the economic choice points in Lesson Three, did the descriptions of each point help you to determine where you are on the scale? What economic conditions have you experienced that brought you to that point? Write your observations here. Remember—don't judge, just observe in a state of neutrality!*

_____

_____

_____

_____

_____

_____

_____

_____

_____

_____

_____

_____

_____

_____

Clarify Your Financial Picture: Gather all of your statements and financial information in one place. Then, use these pages to record your debt, money coming in, money going out, and assets. Add up each column with totals along the bottom.

Past	Present
Debt	**Income**
Total Debt $	**Total Income $**

Notes

Present	Future
Expenses	**Assets**
Total Expenses $	**Total Assets $**

Notes

You may need to add to this list. For example, you may have and need to include student loan debt, childcare payments, or charitable contributions. Make the list as long as it needs to be.

Monthly Bills		Annual Bills
Housing		
Mortgage / Rental	$	
HOA & Maintenance	$	
Utilities	$	
Property Taxes	$	
Housing Total	$	
Transportation		
Loan/Lease	$	
Fuel	$	
Service	$	
Insurance	$	
Transportation Total	$	
Medical		**Annual Total $**
Medical	$	
Dental	$	
Medications	$	
Medical Total	$	
Other		
	$	
	$	
	$	
	$	
Monthly Total	$	

Once you have gathered everything in one place, summarized, and added everything up — take a deep breath and review the numbers. Accept the truth without judgment or scorn. It is what it is. Accept your situation and be proud of yourself for your own personal reconciliation. Remember, this is only one step in your journey. A key part of this work is seeing yourself — not only where you are financially, but also who you are and where you want to go with your life. We are getting to your authentic self. Be sure to save all this information. You'll use it in Lesson 5, of the PACT process, "Taking Action."

Accept Reality and Awaken your Authenticity: Respond to the following questions to see how your past affects the decisions you make today. Be honest and keep drilling down to provide more details wherever you can. Go beyond a simple yes or no. If you get stuck, ask yourself — "What else?"

♥ *What was the state of the economy when you were ages 18 through 25, just as you launched yourself as an adult?*

♥ *Were jobs plentiful when you got out of school and started your career?*

♥ *Did you come from a family that provided funds for college, or did you come out of school with loads of debt?*

♥ *Did you have a great support system—physically, financially, and emotionally—to be exactly who you were drawn to be? Or were you told you were not enough or weren't the right version?*

♥ *Besides student loan debt, how were your other debt levels from car, credit cards, or mortgage debt when you were mid-career? Where do those debts stand now?*

_____

_____

_____

_____

♥ *Did you regret your choice of degree, or never get one and wanted one? Did you succumb to what you "should have" gotten your degree in, or did you study exactly what you actually desired?*

_____

_____

_____

_____

♥ *What else was going on in your world, on a macro or micro level, that impacted your decision-making process as a young adult?*

_____

_____

_____

_____

Reflect: *Carefully consider each of your responses. Are you still making decisions today because you "should" do something or because you really want to? Are you only choosing what's financially prudent while avoiding living in the present moment? Do you feel guilty if you choose something your heart desires? Take a thoughtful look at how your younger years have impacted you today. Now choose. Tell yourself, "I'm going to live a guilt-free life."*

4 Lesson Four Activities
Choosing to Change

Your intentions are the trigger for change. *They are the most powerful tool you can use in wealth building. Turning your heart's desires and dreams into intentions is a spiritual process that opens doors to infinite possibilities. Universal energies interact, combine, and assist, molecule by molecule, atom by atom, to manifest your plans.*

Complete the phrase, "I Choose to…"
This is about you choosing your life from a place of empowerment.

I Choose to…

_____
_____
_____
_____

I Choose to…

_____
_____
_____
_____

I Choose to…

_____
_____
_____
_____

I Choose to…

_____
_____
_____
_____

This exercise will explore your behavioral patterns. *Write responses to the following questions as you work through Lesson Four:*

♥ *How do you go about getting your needs met?*

_____

_____

_____

_____

_____

♥ *How do you or don't you go about taking on responsibility?*

_____

_____

_____

_____

_____

♥ *How do you handle stressful situations?*

_____

_____

_____

_____

_____

♥ *How do you think objectively?*

_____

_____

_____

_____

_____

♥ *How do you do creative brainstorming?*

_____

_____

_____

_____

_____

♥ *What is your behavior like when you've had a recent success?*

_____

_____

_____

_____

_____

♥ *How do you make large purchases?*

_____

_____

_____

_____

_____

Reflect: *Read over your narrative. Can you see yourself following one or more specific behaviors when you try to get what you want? Are the behaviors healthy or harmful? Are they Scarcity or abundant actions? Don't over-think this. Simply ask yourself, "What are my habitual patterns?" This is not about good or bad, right or wrong. It's just something for you to recognize and think about, without self-judgment.*

_____

_____

_____

_____

*Use this space to write down some ideas for overcoming
a lack of "enough" money:*

_____

_____

_____

_____

_____

_____

_____

_____

_____

_____

Use this space to jot down your wants versus your needs:

Wants	Needs

*Use this space to think of and write down names
for your intentional savings accounts:*

_____

_____

_____

_____

If you carry credit card balances, try the "all-cash" method for two months and write down everything you spend here. Then compare it to your previous two months of credit card bills:

Month 1	Month 2
$	$
$	$
$	$
$	$
$	$
$	$
$	$
$	$
$	$
$	$
$	$
$	$
$	$
$	$
$	$
$	$
$	$

Shifting Negative Emotions: Write each emotion or issue you most want to heal in this moment on a separate piece of paper. Ask yourself, "What is my unmet need?" Eventually, something will pop. Whatever it is, feel the feelings as they come up. This is where the healing begins. As you write, you are bringing your feelings about this emotion to the surface, shining light on it to feel and heal it. Then crumple up the paper and throw it away. Even better, burn it. By doing this, you are choosing to distance yourself from old, stagnant energy. This symbolic process allows you to internalize this dramatic event and feel what it's like to be done with negativity. By watching it burn, the emotion, fear, or limiting belief is symbolically removed from your life by choice.

Dissipating Your Fears: Use this space to reflect upon your experience of completing the exercise of lying down in a darkened room and concentrating on your breathing to help you come to terms with your emotions and fears. While breathing, ask yourself questions like, "Why am I sad? What am I afraid of?" Allow these emotions to come to the surface and face the feelings.

Write down your thoughts about each step in the WISE Decision Making Model:

What's your
Why? _____

_____

_____

_____

Does it fill your
Intentions? _____

_____

_____

_____

Does this decision
feel *Safe?* _____

_____

_____

_____

As a result, do you
Evolve to where
you want to be? _____

_____

_____

_____

Talk Nice! Think about and write down one specific thing you do or say to yourself that you want to stop. Be mindful of how you speak to yourself and decide what you will change this week. Making only one adjustment at a time will help make it a more permanent, internalized change. It's easy to decide what will work for you. Maybe it's taking a step forward or backward, clapping your hands, or saying, "No more!" The physicality of the movement helps you break habitual mental patterns.

Your Career Path: Use this space to reflect on your job and your employer. Is your current job the right one for you, or is it time to move on? Remember, don't be limited by thinking you have to stay in any given job, especially when it no longer provides you with what you need or desire.

Limiting Beliefs: The most common words associated with limiting beliefs are "I can't," "I won't," "I don't," "I am not," and "Others might not." Think about whether or not you have limiting beliefs, and write about ways that you can turn them around into positive affirmations.

Turn Your Passion into Reality: Write down your answers to this question: "What things would you like to do but feel you'll never have sufficient money to make happen?" Under each item, write down the specific reason you think you don't have the money you need. Then, reframe your reason to be more positive, using affirmative language.

I'd like to... _____

I can't because... _____

I will because... _____

_____

_____

I'd like to... _____

I can't because... _____

I will because... _____

_____

_____

I'd like to... _____

I can't because... _____

I will because... _____

_____

_____

I'd like to... _____

I can't because... _____

I will because... _____

_____

_____

Gratitude: Shift your vibration higher by writing down what you're grateful for, or who you're grateful for in your life. Make this part of your daily routine by starting here.

I'm grateful for... _____
_____
_____

I'm grateful for... _____
_____
_____

I'm grateful for... _____
_____
_____

I'm grateful for... _____
_____
_____

I'm grateful for... _____
_____
_____

I'm grateful for... _____
_____
_____

Do Right by Yourself: If you are in emotional pain, something is wrong. Emotions are a sign of unmet needs. Think about and write down any needs that are not being met. Then reflect on how you can make a change.

Lesson Five Activities
Taking Action

Use these spaces to record your answers to the questions asked in the first part of Lesson Five. *The responses you provide will reveal trends in stages. Don't try understanding it while doing it — just record every answer to each question and then go back through the list, adding details as they come to you. Consider your answers to these questions in light of what you discovered about yourself in previous lessons. Recognize possibilities to bridge from one side to the other. As your intuition begins giving you hints, write them down.*

My Finances and Debt

Prioritizing payments

Have you prioritized your expenses and debt payoff? If not, please do so.

_____

_____

My short-term emergency reserve

Do you have one? Are you funding it? What do you choose?

_____

_____

The end of my mortgage payments

Have you decided at what age you no longer want mortgage debt? If not, make it a conscious choice.

_____

_____

Amount of debt

Are you comfortable with your debts? Debts represent a lack of freedom and choices in the present moment. Is that what you want?

_____

_____

Children and Family

My Children: Are you allowing your children to drain your cash flow? Do you choose to continue allowing them to do that? Are those the values you want to teach them? Do you need to create healthier boundaries with your children and the way they spend your money? Do you want to pay for your children's college educations? If so, do you think they will attend an in-state, out-of-state, or private university? How much of that cost can you bear?

_____

_____

_____

_____

_____

My Parents: Are you, or will you be, fiscally responsible for your parents? If they require long-term care, are you willing to pay for it or become the caretaker? Will your finances allow for this? It's either your time or your money—but it's your choice.

_____

_____

_____

_____

My Other Family Members: If you have no children, are there people in your life—nieces, nephews, godchildren—who are really important to you? Do you want to contribute anything to their college funding?

_____

_____

_____

_____

Spending and Expenses

Financial Story: What do you want your financial story to be?
Are you spending money in ways that are relevant to you today?

_____
_____
_____
_____
_____
_____
_____
_____
_____

Periodic Expenses: What are the periodic
expenses that throw your cash flow for a loop? Do you
want to create a plan for the surprises or known annual expenses that occur?

_____
_____
_____
_____
_____
_____

Gifting: Is gifting important to you—with your time or your money?

_____
_____
_____
_____
_____

Wealth and Retirement

Retirement Amount: What's your number? How much is enough when building your wealth? Is it based on income or asset level or both?

_____

_____

_____

_____

_____

_____

_____

Retirement Savings Level: How do you feel about your retirement savings level?

_____

_____

_____

_____

_____

Taxes: Are you minimizing the taxes you owe with the investments you currently hold? If you're not sure, do you want to consult with a tax specialist?

_____

_____

_____

_____

_____

_____

Paperwork and Products

Legal Documents: When was the last time you had your legal documents updated or put together? Is it time to take a look?

_____

_____

_____

_____

Current Financial Products: What are the current financial products you have? Do the financial products you hold today support your current financial intentions?

_____

_____

_____

_____

Insurance: If you have life insurance, does that satisfy your needs? Are you aware of what your employer covers for disability insurance? Keep in mind, if your employer pays for your disability insurance premium costs, then the benefit is taxable to you. Meaning you will go home with less money than you think. Will that net tax amount meet your monthly expenses? If not, do you want to consider a supplemental disability plan? Is it important to you?

_____

_____

_____

_____

_____

_____

List Your Debt: Use the information you collected in Lesson 3 to fill in this chart

Debt, with Highest Interest Rate First
1
2
3
4
5
6
7
8
9
10
11
12
13
14

Instructions:

1. Prioritize your debts from top to bottom with the highest interest rate on top of the sheet.

2. Write down the minimum monthly payment on all of them, except the one that has the highest interest rate.

3. Take the total of the actual payments you make monthly on all debts and subtract the minimums on all but the highest rated one.

4. Take the answer from #3 and pay that large, lump sum every month on the highest interest debt until it is gone.

5. Once the first debt is paid off, take that lump-sum monthly payment and apply it to the debt that is next in line, the second highest interest-rate debt.

Rate %	Current Balance	Current Payment	Minimum Payment
	$	$	$
	$	$	$
	$	$	$
	$	$	$
	$	$	$
	$	$	$
	$	$	$
	$	$	$
	$	$	$
	$	$	$
	$	$	$
	$	$	$
	$	$	$
	$	$	$
Totals	$	$	$

Current — Minimum = $

Notes

Additional Strategies for Taking Action

Current Cash Flow: Reflect on the idea of not using debit and credit cards for at least six months to a year. Doing this will help you internalize what you spend and makes money a real, physical thing.

_____

_____

_____

_____

The Bucket System: Use this space for writing out a plan for working with the dollars you have to systematically drop what money you can into buckets— Short-Term, Mid-Term, and Long-Term financial intentions.

_____

_____

_____

_____

_____

Emotional Spending: List times that you may have overspent on items because of an emotional experience. Then think about how you may have resist-ed that urge if you had used cash instead of credit.

_____

_____

_____

_____

_____

Boost Your Cash Flow: Use this space to write down ideas for tweaking your spending habits and energizing your life with the money you have after studying the top 10 quickest ways to increase positive cash flow.

Making Your Dream List Work for You: Make a Dream List. Stop and ponder the things you've always wanted to do that haven't happened yet. Feel the excitement welling up inside as you write them down and begin to make them happen. When you fulfill your first round of dreams, move on to the next one. When your lists are in place, create a timeline that will chart your accomplishments six months, a year, and five years down the road.

Make a Date: Initiate "financial date nights" so that you and your spouse can make sure you are both on the same wave length in regards to funding and prioritizing your mutual goals. At least once a year, use this space to rewrite your Dream List for your family together. Address these five subjects: financial, personal, spiritual, family, and career.

www.ingramcontent.com/pod-product-compliance
Lightning Source LLC
Chambersburg PA
CBHW040910210326
41597CB00029B/5039